Countries of the World

Egypt

Selina Wood

Jere L. Bacharach and Usama Soltan, Consultants

NATIONAL GEOGRAPHIC
WASHINGTON, D.C.

Contents

Foreword

In many people's minds, Egypt has always been tied with ancient civilization. The Nile River has nourished life and civilization in the country for centuries. The glorious Giza Pyramids and the Great Sphinx have been standing in the desert for thousands of years. The Valley of the Kings and the great temples in the southern part of the country still fill visitors with awe. Millions of people have marveled at ancient artifacts and antiquities in the Egyptian Museum in downtown Cairo or in Egyptian collections in other museums around the world.

In this book you will learn about this great country and all these aspects of its glorious civilization. You will also learn about the special place of Egypt in world history due to its geographical location. It has long been a target for near neighbors and distant invaders, from the Greeks and Romans in ancient times to Napoleon Bonaparte's military expedition in the early 19th century and a 70-year-long occupation by British colonialists in modern times.

But there is more to Egypt than mere history. Its ancient glory is just one face of a country that is trying hard to keep up with the progress and development going on around the world. This book will introduce you to modern life in Egypt: its industry, education, arts, sports, politics, and other cultural activities. It will help correct some of the common but often mistaken stereotypes about the country: Egyptians do not ride camels as a means of transportation; many Egyptian women reach a high level of education; and few children work on farms at a young age.

The image of a country with a magnificent past, striving hard to improve the present, and optimistically looking ahead to a bright future

for upcoming generations sometimes makes Egypt a land of contradictions. But this is not necessarily a negative thing: After all, Egyptians have already made successful efforts to improve prospects for our children. In a developing country, this has not always proved easy—but most Egyptians remain hopeful about the future and what it holds for them.

▲ A young Egyptian searches for a present in the window of a Cairo general store.

Usama Soltan, Ph.D.
Visiting Instructor of Arabic
Middlebury College, Vermont

The River
in the
Desert

TRAVELERS ON THE NILE pass between lush green banks lined with reeds and date palms. Most Egyptians live close to the river, which flows from south to north through the length of the country. In the countryside, the Nile provides water to irrigate fields of cotton, rice, sugarcane, wheat, and vegetables. In the cities, promenades along the riverbank are popular spots for families to picnic or take a walk, and for anglers to fish. Yet just a stone's throw away from the river in much of Egypt rises a desert where few plants grow and few people can survive. Egypt depends on the Nile for its existence. Without it, the land would be uninhabitable. But ancient monuments along the river show that it has supported civilizations here for thousands of years.

◄ **Desert hills rise just beyond the banks of the Nile. From outer space, the river valley looks like a thin ribbon of green across the sandy land on either side.**

WHAT'S THE WEATHER LIKE?

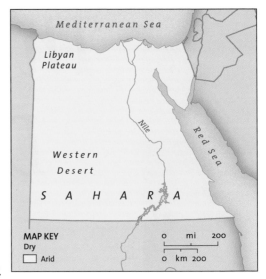

Egypt is hot and dry all year round, although temperatures fall during the winter. The highest rainfall is in the north, on the Mediterranean coast, but even there rain falls only a few times a year. Rainwater quickly evaporates in the hot sun.

It is hottest in the south, near the city of Aswan, where summer temperatures can be a scorching 122° F (50° C). The map opposite shows the physical features of Egypt. Labels on this map and on similar maps throughout this book identify places pictured in each chapter.

Fast Facts

OFFICIAL NAME: Arab Republic of Egypt
FORM OF GOVERNMENT: Republic
CAPITAL: Cairo
POPULATION: 78,887, 007
OFFICIAL LANGUAGE: Arabic
MONETARY UNIT: Egyptian pound (EGP), guinay
AREA: 386,662 sq miles (1,001,449 sq km)
BORDERING NATIONS: Libya, Sudan, Israel, Gaza Strip
HIGHEST POINT: Mount Catherine, 8,668 ft (2,642 m)
LOWEST POINT: Qattara Depression, -436 ft (-133 m)
MAJOR MOUNTAIN RANGES: Eastern highlands, Sinai mountains
MAJOR RIVER: Nile

Average Temperature & Rainfall

Average High/Low Temperatures; Yearly Rainfall

Cairo (Central Valley)
82° F (28° C) / 59° F (15° C); 1 in (2.9 cm)

Alexandria (North Coast)
77° F (25° C)/ 63° F (17° C); 7 in (17.8 cm)

Aswan (Southern Valley)
93° F (34° C)/ 66° F (19° C); 0 in (0 cm)

Sharm el Sheikh (Red Sea)
86° F (30° C) / 70° F (21° C); 0.3 in (0.7 cm)

CYPRUS

SYRIA

LEBANON

Mediterranean Sea

ISRAEL

WEST BANK

GAZA STRIP

JORDAN

Europe
Asia
EGYPT
Africa
Indian
Ocean
Atlantic
Ocean

FISHING BOATS,
page 10
AND
IRRIGATED FIELDS,
page 12

Matruh

Alexandria

Port Said

*Nile
Delta*

*Suez
Canal*

*Libyan
Plateau*

NILOMETER,
page 11

Cairo

Giza

Suez

Gulf of Aqaba

Qattara Depression
(lowest point in Egypt)
-436 ft
133 m

*Siwa
Oasis*

Sinai

BEDOUIN
CAMPFIRE,
page 14

SAINT CATHERINE'S
MONASTERY,
page 15

Mt. Catherine
(Highest point in Egypt)
8,668 ft
2,642 m

Mt. Sinai
7,496 ft
2,285 m

SAUDI
ARABIA

Sharm el Sheikh

CORAL REEF,
page 15

*Farafra
Oasis*

E G Y P T

EL QASR,
page 13

El Qasr

RIVER AND
RUINS,
page 10

Western

*Dakhla
Oasis*

*Kharga
Oasis*

Desert

Luxor

*Red
Sea*

Eastern Desert

Nile

Gulf of Suez

Nile

*Libyan
Desert*

S A H A R A

Aswan High Dam

Aswan

TROPIC OF CANCER

*Lake
Nasser*

SUDAN

MAP KEY

⊛ National capital

● Selected city

+ Elevation

0 | miles | 200

0 | km | 200

Physical Map

▲ Cruise ships carry tourists to ancient sites like the temple at Luxor (right), which all stand close to the Nile.

▼ Fishers use rowing boats and traditional nets to fish on the Nile.

Life-Giving Waters

Without the Nile, Egypt would all be as barren as the desert. No more than an inch (2.5 cm) of rain falls in a year, and in the south rainfall might only be half an inch (1.2 cm) in five years. But each summer, the Nile rises because of rains at its source far to the south, in Ethiopia. Its waters are so dark with soil washed

downstream that the ancient Egyptians called the river Ar or Aur, meaning "Black." Since ancient times, the yearly floods have covered the valley with fertile sediment needed for growing crops.

The river has other uses. In ancient times,

MEASURING THE NILE

For millennia until the late 1900s, the Egyptians depended on nilometers to measure the river and predict the size of the annual flood. If there was too little flooding, water would not reach the farmers' irrigated fields, while too much flooding would wash whole fields of crops away. Ancient and medieval Egyptian society depended on a good harvest—and officials also wanted to calculate how much tax farmers had to pay to the rulers.

Beginning in ancient times, nilometers were built along the river. They came in two forms. Some were vertical columns with interval marks against which the water could be measured as it rose. Others were tanks with steps leading down into the water, with depth markings on the walls.

▲ The nilometer on Rawdah Island, Cairo

Nile boats carried goods such as gold. Today the Nile irrigates the land and is still a busy transportation route. Most of Egypt's major towns and cities stand on its banks; so do the pyramids and other ancient sites. Many tourists travel between sites on cruise ships.

The Nile is the world's longest river, flowing over 3,980 miles (6,400 km) through eastern Africa, Sudan, and Egypt. Today its flow is controlled by the High Dam in Aswan in southern Egypt, to help farmers manage the irrigation of their crops.

OASES

I n parts of the Egyptian desert, underground water lies close to the surface. The water is carried in layers of rock called aquifers, and may have originated hundreds of miles away. Places where aquifers rise to the surface are called oases. The springs provide water in the desert for animals and crops, and attract settlers. One of the largest oases is Dakhla, far west of Luxor, which today has a population of more than 70,000 people. Many desert nomads have stopped moving around and settled at oases. They can enjoy the benefits of modern life, such as electricity, schools, and healthcare.

▼ **A donkey turns a pump to water fields in the Nile Delta.**

A Fertile Valley

Egypt is often divided into two sections—Upper Egypt lies in the south, from the Sudanese border to the capital, Cairo; in the north, Lower Egypt stretches from Cairo to the Mediterranean Sea. The names can be confusing, because "lower" in geography usually means "to the south." In Egypt, the terms refer to the course of the Nile, the only major river in the world that flows from south to north.

In Upper Egypt, the river runs through a narrow valley between low mountains that mark the edge of the desert. In the plains of Lower Egypt, the valley is wider, on average 6 miles (10 km) across. North of Cairo, the river splits into a triangular delta of many channels. Farmers here use pumps and canals to irrigate their crops, so almost every inch of land is covered with fields of beans, vegetables, and fruit such as grapes and bananas. On the edge of the delta stands the port of

Alexandria, Egypt's second-largest city and a busy center for industries such as food processing and automobile assembly. The government is encouraging Egypt's industries to reduce the amount of smoke or fumes they create. Cairo is often covered in a haze caused by pollution from cars and factories mixed with dust from the desert.

▲ Since the time of the pharaohs, the town of El Qasr at the Dakhla oasis has been an important center for traders crossing the desert.

Seas of Sand

West of the Nile lies part of the Sahara Desert that stretches across North Africa. This Western Desert covers two-thirds of Egypt's land. In spring and summer a hot wind blows east out of the desert, drying up everything in its path. Egyptians hate the

AT HOME IN THE DESERT

Although few Bedouin still live as nomads, their ancestors wandered Egypt's deserts for centuries. They were at home in a harsh landscape that might have meant death for other people. The Bedouin traveled great distances to find scrub for their animals to eat. In the Western Desert, they found their way across sand dunes that changed in the wind. Roars and hums from within the dunes echo across the desert. Scientists think this "singing" is caused when sand grains within the dune all vibrate at the same time. It sounds a little like an aircraft engine.

The Bedouin navigated by the position of the stars and the changing dunes, and by following desert animals between oases.

▼ **The Sinai Desert is rockier than the sandy Western Desert and can be tough to navigate.**

wind, which whips up dust and sand that turn the sun deep orange. They call the wind *khamsin*, from the Arabic word for "fifty"—it usually blows for about fifty days, while everyone waits for it to end. The nomadic Bedouin believed that the khamsin made people crazy.

Bedouin law excused some crimes committed while it was blowing. In the desert, the Bedouin wear robes and scarves to protect them from the sand and dust.

Mountains and Sea

East of the Nile, the rocky plateau of the Eastern Desert extends to the Red Sea. The water is clear and blue, and no one is sure how the sea got its name. It may come from blooms of reddish algae. Beyond the Red Sea is the Sinai Desert, a stony plain. The central mountains of the Sinai contain Egypt's highest point, Mount Catherine. The mountain's peak is covered with snow in winter. Better known is Mount Sinai (7,496 ft; 2,285 m). According to the Bible, Moses climbed this mountain to receive the Ten Commandments from God.

▲ Saint Catherine's monastery was built at the foot of Mount Sinai.

▼ Coral in the Red Sea

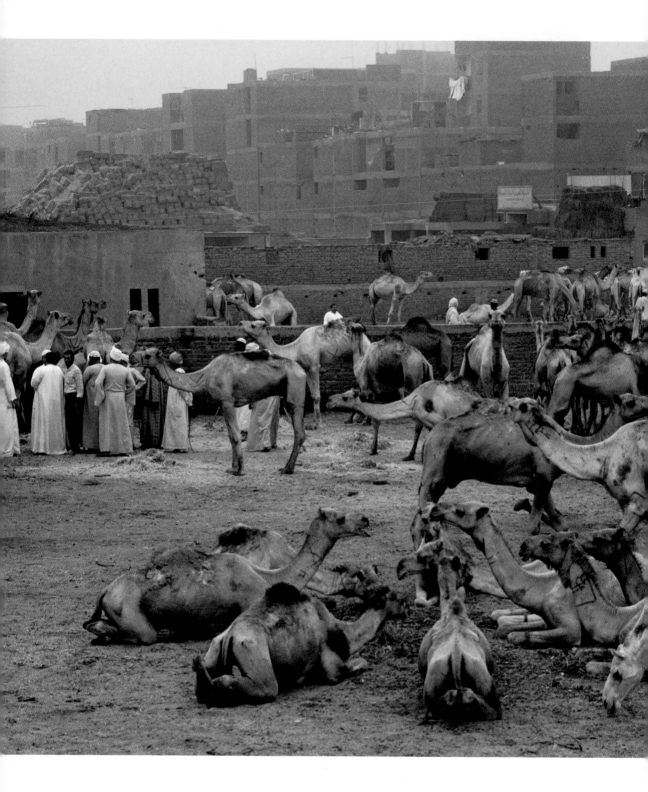

Riches
in the
Desert

THE EGYPTIANS HAVE ALWAYS been close to the natural world. Ancient Egyptians believed that the jackal was sacred. One of their gods—Anubis—had a jackal's head. They mummified animals after their deaths just as they did important people. The Egyptians were also one of the first peoples to raise livestock and keep cats as pets. Later, one of the most important domesticated animals in Egypt was the camel, which is called the "ship of the desert." Like ships, they carried people and goods. Camels can survive for long periods without water by living off fat stores in their humps. Camels also provided meat, milk, wool, and skins. Today, they are most often used to give rides to tourists or for camel racing, a popular sport in Egypt.

◀ Camels, here at the market in Cairo, have been a part of desert life in Egypt since at least the Islamic conquest in the sixth century.

PROTECTED PARADISES

The best places to see Egypt's wildlife are its 21 protected regions, which include oases, deserts, mountains, coastal areas, river islands, and wetlands. Perhaps the most surprising is Ras Mohammed National Park on the Sinai coast. One of the biggest and oldest of Egypt's national parks, it contains a wealth of marine life, including sharks.

The map opposite shows vegetation zones—or what grows where—in Egypt. Vegetation zones form ecosystems, or environments that support specific plant and animal life. Egypt is home to a wide variety of animals and plants. It is a particularly good place to see interesting birds, many of which visit on their annual migration.

▶ A female Nile crocodile carries her newly-hatched babies in her mouth. The crocodile is now rare in Egypt but can be found in countries in sub-Saharan Africa.

Species at Risk

A number of species in Egypt are losing their natural habitats. The deserts are shrinking as people irrigate their edges. In the past few hundred years, other native animals have become extinct through hunting. The Egyptians are trying to help endangered species by creating protected regions, although the government lacks the funds and resources to run many large-scale national parks.

The species below are among those at risk:

> White-headed duck
> Striped hyena
> Sand cat
> Saker falcon
> Cheetah
> Nile crocodile
> Greater spotted eagle
> Egyptian tortoise
> Nubian ibex

> Cinereous vulture
> Houbara bustard (bird)
> Dorcas gazelle
> Golden hamster
> Blasius's horseshoe bat
> Dugong
> Dalmation pelican
> Cape shark

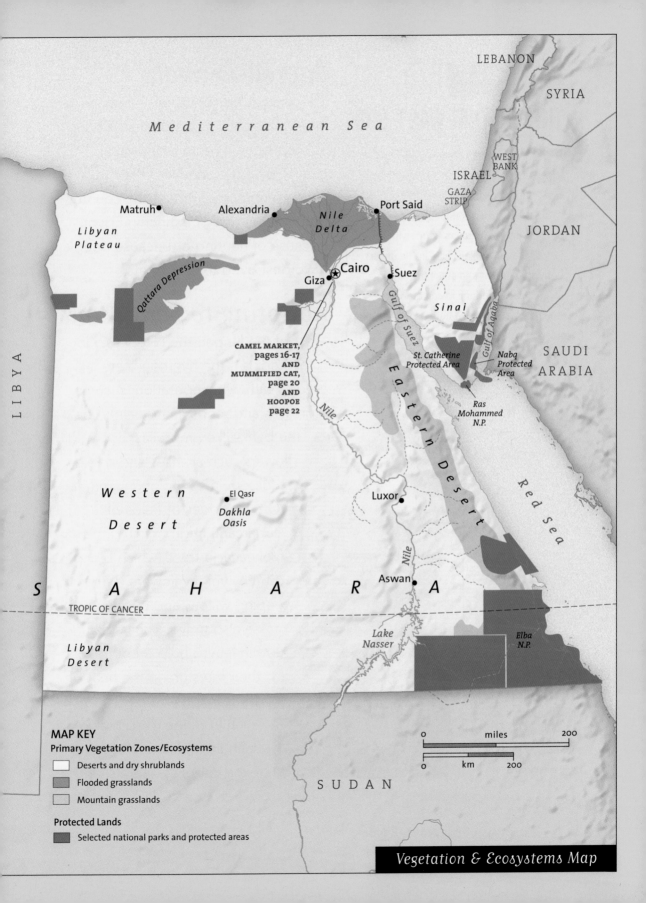

LEBANON

SYRIA

Mediterranean Sea

Matruh ●

Alexandria ●

Nile Delta

Port Said ●

ISRAEL

WEST BANK

GAZA STRIP

JORDAN

Libyan Plateau

Qattara Depression

Giza ● ⊛ Cairo

● Suez

Sinai

Gulf of Suez

Gulf of Aqaba

St. Catherine Protected Area

Nabq Protected Area

SAUDI ARABIA

CAMEL MARKET,
pages 16-17
AND
MUMMIFIED CAT,
page 20
AND
HOOPOE
page 22

Nile

Ras Mohammed N.P.

Red Sea

_W e s t e r n_

El Qasr ●

Dakhla Oasis

_D e s e r t_

Luxor ●

_E a s t e r n   D e s e r t_

Nile

S   A   H   A   R   A

Aswan ●

TROPIC OF CANCER

Libyan Desert

Lake Nasser

Elba N.P.

S U D A N

MAP KEY
Primary Vegetation Zones/Ecosystems

▢ Deserts and dry shrublands

▢ Flooded grasslands

▢ Mountain grasslands

Protected Lands

▢ Selected national parks and protected areas

LIBYA

0 ___ miles ___ 200

0 ___ km ___ 200

Vegetation & Ecosystems Map

THE DOG THAT WAS A GOD

The ancient Egyptians called the jackal "the howler" because of the mournful singing sounds it makes at nightfall. They worshiped the dog in the form of Anubis, a human figure with a jackal's head. Jackals lived in the desert but visited towns and cities to scavenge for food, often lurking in cemeteries. Anubis was worshiped both as the guardian of cemeteries and the god who oversaw the mummification of the dead.

▶ A mummified cat. Cats became associated with the gods because they helped protect families from pests such as rodents. Statues and mummies of cats were given to temples as sacrifices and buried in huge cemeteries.

Sacred Animals

The ancient Egyptians left paintings and friezes showing large animals such as elephants, hippos, leopards, cheetahs, and crocodiles. They were once plentiful throughout the country but are now rare or extinct in Egypt because of hunting or because people have destroyed their habitats.

Adapting to Conditions

Most of the land in the Nile Valley is cultivated, but the riverbanks are still fringed with wild vegetation, such as grasses and reeds. Date palms line the banks like umbrellas, and wildflowers such as irises and daisies blossom in spring and summer. On the edges of fields of sugarcane and banana groves grow acacia trees, which bloom with tiny yellow flowers. Tamarisk, weeping willow, and eucalyptus trees also thrive. Their small, thin leaves help them to keep their moisture in the heat of the sun.

Out in the desert, animals such as wild cats, desert foxes, gazelles, jackals, and hyenas have developed different ways of coping with the conditions. The fennec fox, for instance, loses heat through its large ears and hides in a burrow during the day. It comes out at night, when the air is much cooler, to hunt insects and small animals. Desert animals get most of the water they need from the small amounts they find in their food.

A REALLY USEFUL PLANT

The papyrus plant—a long reed that once grew along the banks of the Nile—was vital for the ancient Egyptians. Its fibers were used to make tough cloth and rope, and to bind together wood to make boats. It also provided an early form of writing material, made by cutting the pith of a papyrus stem into strips, pressing the strips together, and drying them in a thin sheet. Papyrus no longer grows in Egypt but can be found in countries such as Sudan and Uganda.

▲ This ancient papyrus includes a plan of a royal tomb and discussions about building tombs.

Watch Out!

Throughout history, Egyptians have feared poisonous animals, many of which live in the desert just beyond human communities. They include venomous snakes like the cobra and the horned viper, and scorpions. The Egyptian queen Cleopatra was said to use a poisonous snake named an asp to commit suicide. Scorpions rest under stones during the day and mostly come out at night. A scorpion's curled tail carries a powerful stinger.

Bird Paradise

The rivers, wetlands, and deserts of Egypt are home to more than 400 species of birds. Many birds stop over on the migration from northern Europe to the south of Africa for the winter. Egypt is their first chance to rest after flying across the Mediterranean Sea. In the deserts, birds of prey such as eagles and falcons search for food; along the river and in the delta swamps, kingfishers, pelicans, and cranes catch fish. One of the most distinctive Egyptian birds, the hoopoe, has striking black and white wings, a long down-curved bill, and a large crest that it extends when it is excited.

▶ With its distinctive markings and crest, the hoopoe is an easily recognizable visitor to Egyptian gardens.

Continuing Complexity

The relationship between Egyptians and animals is complex. Some wild species are declining in numbers as their habitat is destroyed. The rapid tourist development of the Red Sea coast is disturbing life on the coral reefs. But the remote parts of the desert still provide safe areas for wildlife such as the Dorcas gazelle and the ibex. Meanwhile, domesticated animals such as camels, sheep, and goats live closely with the people who depend on them.

▲ Male ibex fight with their curved horns.

▼ The jackal scavenges at the edge of the desert.

Millennia
on the
Nile

ON THE OUTSKIRTS OF CAIRO, Egyptians come face to face with their ancient history. Just across the Nile rise the towering pyramids of Giza. The pyramids were built by the people that dominated the Nile valley and delta beginning in the third millennium B.C. The great structures were tombs for kings called pharaohs, whom the Egyptians treated like gods. Today, the pyramids are the most familiar symbol of Egypt. There is far more to Egyptian history, however. Clearly visible from the pyramids rise the domes and minarets of Cairo's mosques, or Islamic places of worship. These are monuments of a far more recent golden age. Only about a thousand years ago, Egypt was the cultural and trading center of the medieval Islamic world.

◀ **A camel rider looks over the pyramids at Giza. The Great Pyramid of Khufu (right, in the distance) is probably the largest single structure ever built by humans.**

THE FIRST FARMERS

The first people to live on the banks of the Nile were hunters and fishers, who settled there over 8,000 years ago. In time, the Nile people discovered how to grow crops of wild wheat and barley in the fertile mud left by the river's annual flood, or inundation. They bred special kinds of wheat and barley that yielded more grains. Later they also began to keep sheep, goats, and cattle.

Villages sprang up along the river, and people discovered how to mine gold and precious stones in the desert. They built towns and made expeditions to trade with other communities in Africa and West Asia. They sailed up and down the Nile and along the Mediterranean coast to neighboring cultures. Protected from invaders by the surrounding desert, by 3000 B.C. these Nile people had developed a wealthy, distinctive civilization.

▲ Emmer wheat was one of the first crops to be farmed by Egyptians and remains an important source of food today.

Time line

This chart shows the approximate dates for the major periods of Ancient Egypt.

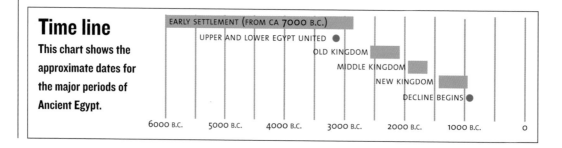

EARLY SETTLEMENT (FROM CA 7000 B.C.)

UPPER AND LOWER EGYPT UNITED ●

OLD KINGDOM

MIDDLE KINGDOM

NEW KINGDOM

DECLINE BEGINS ●

| 6000 B.C. | 5000 B.C. | 4000 B.C. | 3000 B.C. | 2000 B.C. | 1000 B.C. | 0 |

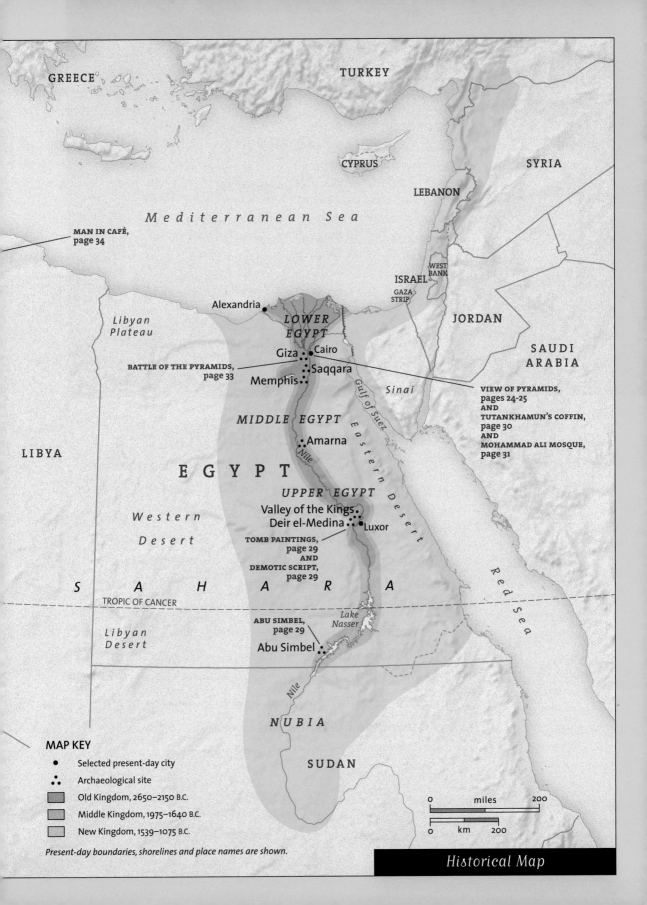

GREECE

TURKEY

Mediterranean Sea

CYPRUS

LEBANON

SYRIA

MAN IN CAFÉ,
page 34

WEST
BANK

ISRAEL

GAZA
STRIP

JORDAN

SAUDI
ARABIA

Alexandria

*Libyan
Plateau*

LOWER
EGYPT

Giza

Cairo

BATTLE OF THE PYRAMIDS,
page 33

Saqqara

Memphis

Gulf of Suez

Sinai

VIEW OF PYRAMIDS,
pages 24-25
AND
TUTANKHAMUN'S COFFIN,
page 30
AND
MOHAMMAD ALI MOSQUE,
page 31

LIBYA

MIDDLE EGYPT

Amarna

Nile

E G Y P T

Eastern Desert

UPPER EGYPT

*Western

Desert*

Valley of the Kings
Deir el-Medina

Luxor

TOMB PAINTINGS,
page 29
AND
DEMOTIC SCRIPT,
page 29

S A H A R A

Red Sea

TROPIC OF CANCER

*Lake
Nasser*

*Libyan
Desert*

ABU SIMBEL,
page 29

Abu Simbel

Nile

N U B I A

SUDAN

MAP KEY

● Selected present-day city

⋮ Archaeological site

▮ Old Kingdom, 2650–2150 B.C.

▮ Middle Kingdom, 1975–1640 B.C.

▮ New Kingdom, 1539–1075 B.C.

Present-day boundaries, shorelines and place names are shown.

0   miles   200

0   km   200

Historical Map

Magnificent Civilization

Around 3100 B.C., the kingdoms of Upper and Lower Egypt were unified under a powerful king, later called a pharaoh. Under the pharaohs that followed, the Egyptians built magnificent pyramids, temples, and other monuments. They also conquered new lands, including Nubia (modern Sudan) to the south, and Palestine and Syria to the northeast.

Pharaohs had to pay the workers who labored on their building programs. It was an expensive business, because there were many gods who required monuments. The pharaohs had to employ engineers to design the buildings and craftsmen to decorate them. They had complex systems to raise taxes to fund the works.

THE CULT OF THE DEAD

Much of Egyptian life was concerned with death. The Egyptians believed that each person had a life force, or *ka.* The ka lived on after death in a land much like Egypt, as long as it had a home and was properly cared for. Corpses were preserved by skilled workers who made them into mummies by drying them and wrapping them in cloth. Mummies were buried in tombs with belongings to use in the Afterlife, and with spells to protect themselves. It was not only pharaohs and other rulers who had elaborate burials. In the Middle Kingdom, many wealthy Egyptians were buried in grand tombs, such as pyramids.

▶ Pages from the *Book of the Dead* painted in the tomb of Queen Nefertiti.

The Egyptians were also one of the first peoples to invent a system of writing. It used picture symbols, or hieroglyphics to represent ideas just as we use combinations of letters today. Hieroglyphics were used to write down religious texts and record

▲ The Egyptians used demotic script for quick everyday writing.

◀ This tomb painting shows a wealthy Egyptian woman playing a board game.

TUTANKHAMUN

In November 1922, British archaeologist Howard Carter made a remarkable discovery. In the Valley of the Kings, the royal burial ground near Luxor, Carter discovered an intact tomb. Most ancient tombs had been the victims of robbers, but this one was still sealed. As he peered into the chamber, Carter saw a host of treasures that had been buried with the king for the afterlife. The tomb was that of Tutankhamun, whose mummy was in a solid gold coffin with a stunning death mask. Little is known about Tutankhamun's life; he ruled for only ten years before he died in his late teens in 1323 B.C. Some experts believe that he may have been murdered, but tests on his body have not provided any proof.

▲ Visitors to a Cairo museum admire Tutankhamun's gold sarcophagus, or coffin.

important events. They were slow to write. A much quicker form of writing, called demotic, was used for everyday business.

A Declining Empire

By 1000 B.C., Egypt was in decline. The kingdom had split into smaller parts. Over the centuries strong neighbors emerged to attack and occupy Egyptian territory. In 332 B.C., Egypt was conquered by Alexander the Great of Macedonia. He founded a new city in Egypt, named for himself, Alexandria. The ruling family that succeeded Alexander, the Ptolemies, introduced aspects of Greek culture to Egypt, such as a festival that resembled the Olympic Games. They made Alexandria a wealthy city and a major center of learning.

Roman Rule

The last of the Ptolemies, Queen Cleopatra, was a famous beauty. She won the affection of the Roman general Mark Antony, whom she married. The pair attacked the Roman empire, but were defeated at the Battle of Actium in 31 B.C. Egypt fell under Roman control. The Romans sent most of Egypt's agricultural produce such as wheat to feed its own citizens. At first the Egyptians were free to worship their ancient gods, but in A.D. 323 the Romans made Christianity the official religion of the empire and shut down the old temples. Ancient Egyptian culture was finally lost, although Alexandria remained an important city. The Egyptian Christians established the Coptic tradition, which still survives today.

Warriors of Islam

In A.D. 640, mounted Muslim warriors from the Arabian peninsula swept into Egypt, founding a city that later became known as Cairo. The newcomers' faith, Islam, became Egypt's dominant religion. For centuries, the region was ruled by various Islamic dynasties, many of which were not of Egyptian origin.

▲ A Coptic monk with a painting of Saint Anthony. Anthony spent twenty years as a hermit in the Egyptian desert before founding the world's first monastery.

◀ The Muhammad Ali mosque dominates the Citadel, the walled part of Cairo that was home to the city's rulers for 700 years.

History   **31**

In 1250, the new rulers were called Mamluks. They were slaves who had been trained as elite warriors; now they seized power in Egypt and around the east coast of the Mediterranean. For two and a half centuries, Cairo was the cultural heart of the Islamic world and a busy port. In 1517, the Mamluks were defeated by the Ottoman Turks, who made Egypt a

▲ French troops use rifles and cannons to defeat the Mamluks, armed with swords, at the Battle of the Pyramids.

province of their empire. Mamluks took power again at the end of the eighteenth century, but only briefly. Napoleon Bonaparte invaded Egypt and defeated the Malmuks at the Battle of the Pyramids in 1798.

Napoleon's victory was a sign that Egypt was no longer a strong power. It was in danger of becoming isolated and unimportant. The country was ruled by Ottoman Turks, and France and Britain both influenced Egyptian affairs. The rivalry of the European powers would once more make Egypt vital to world politics.

NAPOLEON IN EGYPT

General Napoleon Bonaparte, later emperor of France, invaded Egypt in 1798. France was at war with Britain, and Napoleon aimed to cut Britain's routes to India. The expedition brought few military gains, but had a huge effect on Europeans' view of Egypt. Napoleon brought scholars and artists who studied ancient Egyptian treasures and published their findings in *Description de l'Egypt*, a 24-volume work with 3,000 illustrations. French troops also found the Rosetta Stone, a tablet inscribed in three languages that enabled scholars to decipher hieroglyphics. The breakthrough gave them a greater insight into the ancient civilization and helped spark a new fascination with ancient Egypt across Europe. The stone itself was later taken to London by the British.

▼ Jean-Léon Gérome painted an imaginary image of Napoleon crossing the desert.

British Control

In the middle of the nineteenth century the ruling family of Egypt allowed the French to build a canal to link the Mediterranean Sea and the Red Sea. The 101-mile (160-km) canal cut the shipping route to Asia from Europe, which previously ran around the southern tip of Africa, a trip of 4,000 miles (6,435 km). But by the time the canal opened in 1869, the Egyptian government was bankrupt. It sold its share of the Suez Canal Company to the British, who were eager to control both Egypt and the canal, which was a short route to their colonies in India.

In 1882 the British invaded and occupied Egypt. They continued to control the canal and have great influence in Egypt until 1952, when a group of army officers seized power and declared Egypt a republic.

One of the officers, Colonel Gamal Abdel Nasser, was elected president in 1954. He promised to share Egypt's wealth more fairly. He also said that Egypt would take over the Suez Canal. Britain, France, and Israel sent troops to seize the canal, but retreated when the United Nations and the United States threatened to intervene.

▲ A Libyan sits in a café beneath a portrait of Egypt's President Nasser. Nasser became a hero throughout the Arab world for rejecting foreign influence in Egypt.

War and Peace

The new Egypt also faced conflict with its neighbor, Israel, which had been created in 1948 by international law. Egyptians supported their fellow Arabs, who claimed that Israel stood on territory that rightfully belonged to Arab peoples. The two sides fought a series of wars.

In the 1970s, Egyptian president Anwar Sadat became the first Arab leader to begin negotiations with Israel. The talks led to the historic Camp David peace agreement in 1978, when Sadat acknowleged Israel's right to exist. Other Arab countries disliked the agreement, and Egypt became isolated in the Arabic and Islamic worlds. On October 6, 1981, Sadat was killed by Islamic extremists. He had paid the highest price for his search for peace.

▼ Egyptian President Anwar Sadat (left) joins U.S. President Jimmy Carter (center) and Israel's Prime Minister Menachem Begin in signing the Camp David Accords in 1978. Some Egyptians bitterly resented the deal with the Israelis, whom they saw as the enemies of the Arab peoples.

Festivals
and
Families

EVEN IN A COUNTRY WITH many festivals, the Moulid at Luxor is one of the largest and most lively. Held in honor of the city's patron saint, Abu al-Haggag, the Moulid draws people from all over Egypt to the area around the saint's mosque. They sing and dance to drums, tambourines, and violins. The streets are lined with stalls selling candies and party hats. The crowds watch traditional stick dancing, called *tahtib*. Dancers have to be quick to jump in and out of moving sticks without having their ankles bashed. Another favorite entertainment is *mirmah*, or displays of horse riding. Local festivals take place across Egypt throughout the year. Most of them celebrate some aspect of the Muslim religion (Islam), which is at the heart of everyday life.

◀ Riding tricks during a Moulid are a reminder that the horse has a long history in Egypt, which was one of the first places where people learned to ride the animals.

AN INCREASING POPULATION

Egypt's population stands at nearly 79 million and is growing rapidly. The total is increasing by more than one million a year, and has more than doubled since 1970. Egyptians are starting to have smaller families, thanks in part to a government campaign to encourage parents to have fewer children. However, the tradition is still for families to have five or more children, especially in rural areas. Large families are useful for working on the land. There has also been a sharp fall in the death rate due largely to better health care. Egyptians born today have a life expectancy of seventy-one years. In 1970, it was just under fifty years.

The increase in population has created problems. Most Egyptians live on 5 percent of the land, in the Nile Valley. The rest of the country is nearly empty. Some cities, such as Cairo, have become overcrowded. Many people live close together in small apartments and there are not enough jobs to go around. Schools and hospitals sometimes struggle to cope with all the people. Increased traffic adds to air pollution.

1950 / 21.9 million	1970 / 35.3 million
32% Urban / 68% Rural	42% Urban / 58% Rural
1990 / 55.7 million	**2005 / 74 million**
43% Urban / 57% Rural	42% Urban / 58% Rural

Common Egyptian Phrases

Everyday Egyptian is different from standard Arabic and can be difficult for non-Egyptians to pronounce. There are many glottal stops, or sounds made by closing the throat, which are shown by an apostrophe. Here are a few phrases you might use in Egypt. Give them a try:

Salam alaikum (sa-LAM al-AY-kum)	Hello
Sabah al-khayr (sa-bah al-KAIR)	Good morning
Misa' al-khayr (mees-a' al-KAIR)	Good evening
Ma'as salama (MA'-as sa-LAM-ah)	Goodbye
Shukran (SHOO-kran)	Thank you
'Afwan ('ahf-waan)	You're welcome

LEBANON

SYRIA

Mediterranean Sea

WEST
BANK

ISRAEL

GAZA
STRIP

JORDAN

Matruh

Kafr el Sheikh

Damietta

Damanhur

El Mansura

Port Said

Alexandria

El Arish

Kafr el Dauwar

Tanta

El Mahalla el Kubra

Shibin el Kom

Ismailia

Benha

Zagazig

Shubra el Kheima

Cairo

Suez

SOCCER GAME,
page 45

Sixth of October City

Giza

SUFI WORSHIPERS,
page 41
AND
MOVIE BILLBOARDS,
page 44
AND
SOCCER FANS,
page 45

Helwan

El Faiyum

Beni Suef

Gulf of Suez

Gulf of Aqaba

FARMING
FAMILY,
page 40
AND
DATES AT MARKET,
page 43

El Minya

Mallawi

SAUDI
ARABIA

WOMEN WORKING AT HOME,
page 42

Asyut

Hurghada

Akhmim

Sohag

Quseir

Girga

Qena

CHILDREN'S PROCESSION,
page 42

Luxor

Red Sea

El Kharga

RIDER AT MOULID,
pages 36-37

Idfu

Aswan

TROPIC OF CANCER

LIBYA

SUDAN

MAP KEY

People per square mile		People per square kilometer
Over 2500		Over 1000
625–2498		250–999
62–623		25–249
12–60		5–24
2–11		1–4
Under 2		Under 1

Population of urban area

■ Over 5 million

▲ 1 million to 5 million

● 250,000 to 1 million

• Under 250,000

miles

0   200

0   200
km

Population Map

▲ In rural areas children often help their families in the fields, like this young boy tending sheep with his grandfather.

Islam

About 90 percent of Egyptians are Muslim. Five times a day steets fill with the sound of the muezzin (mosque official) calling Muslims to prayer. In 2005, people in Cairo complained that too many calls to prayer, or *azan*, were broadcast through loudspeakers at slightly different times in different keys. They made an ear-splitting din—especially at dawn. The government said that there should be just one azan, broadcast at the same time from every mosque. But the mosques refused: They said that each azan was unique.

Around 10 percent of Egyptians are Copts. Their church is one of the oldest branches of Christianity. Like other Christians, they hold church services on Sundays and celebrate festivals like Christmas and Easter.

The Family

Egyptians traditionally marry young and have lots of children. The children are close to their families, because aunts and grandparents help to look after them. In rural areas women do most child care and look after the home. After work, men socialize with friends, perhaps playing backgammon in a café. Attitudes are changing, however. City families are smaller, and women are often educated and have jobs. The government is urging girls to stay in school and marry later so that they can begin a career before having children.

NATIONAL HOLIDAYS

Most public holidays in Egypt mark religious festivals, but some commemorate key events in Egypt's history. Everyone celebrates religious holidays, even if they don't follow the particular religion. Individual towns and cities also celebrate their own festivals, usually in honor of a patron saint.

JANUARY 1	New Year's Day
JANUARY 7	Coptic Christmas
MARCH/APRIL	Easter,
	Sham an-Nessim
APRIL 25	Sinai Liberation Day
MAY 1	May Day
JULY 23	Revolution Day
OCTOBER 6	National Day

◀ Members of a Sufi group gather in a mosque in Cairo. Sufism is an ancient form of Islam that emphasizes the mysterious nature of God.

WOMEN AND CHILDREN IN EGYPT

In traditional Islamic societies, men and women have distinct roles. Sometimes women are not allowed out of the home without their husband, or have to wear a veil to go out. In Egypt, the roles tend to be more relaxed. Women are not segregated from everyday life or forced to wear a veil, although many choose to. Children are highly valued. In rural areas they are vital workers on family farms and a great source of security to aging parents—children are expected to look after their parents in old age. In 2006, a third of the population was under 14. The government provides free education up to university level. Many children, however, leave school at the age of about 12 to help in family businesses.

▲ These women combine child care with work at home, weaving baskets to sell to tourists.

▼ Children dressed in traditional costumes take part in a pretend wedding during a festival. Most Egyptians today wear more modern clothes.

Crowded Cairo

Nearly half of Egyptians live in cities and towns. The capital, Cairo, is one of the world's most crowded cities, with a population of at least 18 million. With so many people, it is a noisy and exciting city, with modern skyscrapers rising above medieval mosques.

Many people move to Cairo from rural areas to find jobs. The city is getting so full that the government has built new towns on

the edge of the desert, such as Sixth of October City, 25 miles (40 km) from Cairo.

Flowers for Food

Egypt's food has been shaped by influences from all over, including Persian rice dishes and spices from Asia and North Africa. The Turks who once governed Egypt used flavors made from flowers, such as roses or orange blossoms, which are still popular. In southern Egypt people drink a red tea made from dried hibiscus flowers. Street stalls everywhere sell quick dishes made with local ingredients such as fava beans, eggplants, tomatoes, dates, and nuts with *aish baladi* (bread). Egyptians eat lots of bread, rice, and pasta. Pork is forbidden for Muslims, so chicken and lamb are the

People & Culture   **43**

▲ Billboards of Arabic movie stars decorate a Cairo cinema.

most popular meats. Egyptians prefer eating at home with the family to eating in restaurants, but fast-food chains are very popular. They sell hamburgers, but in Egypt the burgers might be made of falafel—fried vegetables and chickpeas—instead of meat.

From Arts to Sports

Egypt lies at the heart of Arab culture, and Egyptian books and music are popular throughout Arab countries. Egyptian novelists were among the first Arab writers to experiment with modern styles of literature and to achieve international success. In 1988, the Egyptian novelist Naguib Mahfouz became the first Arab to win the Nobel prize for literature.

UMM KULTHUM

Egyptian Umm Kulthum was the most famous Arab singer of the 20th century. Her love songs, which could last hours, were so popular that the streets were deserted when people listened to her radio show. Like other Arabic musicians, she used notes not found in Western music, creating a distinctive sound. At her funeral in 1975, millions of mourners brought Cairo to a standstill.

Cairo is the Hollywood of the Arab world. In the 1940s and 1950s, studios in the city turned out more than 100 movies every year. American blockbusters are more popular now, but Egyptian directors such as Yousef Chahine still make films that are screened at international movie festivals.

Cairo is also a thriving media center, and Egyptian TV shows are broadcast to many Arab countries. The government runs national and regional TV channels, but Egyptians with satellite TV can watch a wide range of channels from all over the region, and even Europe and the United States. Young people like music channels that feature Western bands and Dream-1, an entertainment channel whose news anchor is a former Miss Egypt.

▼ **Children play soccer in a village next to the pyramids at Giza.**

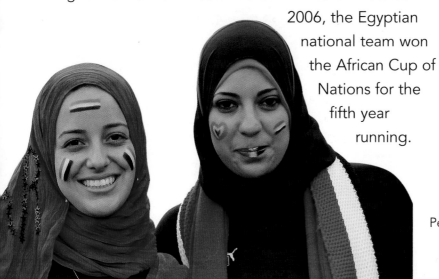

Stop for Soccer

Egypt's favorite sport is soccer. When important matches are being played, the country comes to a standstill and everyone gathers around TV sets in their homes or in stores. In 2006, the Egyptian national team won the African Cup of Nations for the fifth year running.

◀ **These fans at an international soccer game don't just wear scarfs in the team colors with their traditional robes—they paint flags on their faces, too!**

People & Culture **45**

A
Promising Future

I N 1826 THE OTTOMAN SULTAN ordered his male subjects to wear the red fez throughout the empire, including Egypt. The hat was a sign that the empire was changing. The sultan wanted people to stop wearing traditional robes and dress in a more modern way. In Egypt, where the hat is called a *tarboosh*, it remained a lasting symbol of the country long after Egypt became independent of the Ottoman Empire in 1914. It is still popular among the tourists who make up a major part of Egypt's income. Visitors buy the hats as souvenirs, and they are often worn by hotel staff. Today, however, the fez is a symbol of the past, not the future. The textile industry that produced it is still important, but Egypt looks to other industries for economic growth and to political reform.

◀ **A market stall stacked with traditional fezzes in the 12th-century Citadel of Saladin, the fortified area at the heart of Old Cairo.**

GOVERNMENT

Egypt's geography, population, history, and military strength have made it highly influential in the region. Under President Nasser it became a center of pan-Arabism, the belief that Arab nations have common interests. The League of Arab States—a group of countries that cooperate on political, social, and economic issues—is still based in Cairo. Egypt's president has also often chaired the African Union, which aims to boost development throughout Africa.

Egypt is officially a democratic republic. The country is divided into 26 administrative regions or governorates. Authority in the regions is exercised by governors and mayors, who are appointed by the central government, and by councils elected by local people.

▶ Textiles are important exports—and a key part of the home economy. Cotton, being picked here in the 1950s, was only introduced in the 19th century; ancient Egyptians wore linen, made from flax.

Trading Partners

Egypt's major trading partners are members of the European Union and the United States. Its chief exports are oil and gas, textiles, metals, household appliances, and chemical products. Its imports include equipment for making industrial machines, food, chemicals, wood products, and fuels.

Country	Percentage Egypt Exports
Italy	11.9%
United States	10.8%
United Kingdom	7.0%
Syria	6.6%
Germany	4.7%
Spain	4.2%
All others combined	54.8%

Country	Percentage Egypt Imports
United States	12.2%
Germany	7.0%
Italy	6.6%
France	5.6%
China	5.4%
United Kingdom	4.7%
Saudi Arabia	4.1%
All others combined	54.4%

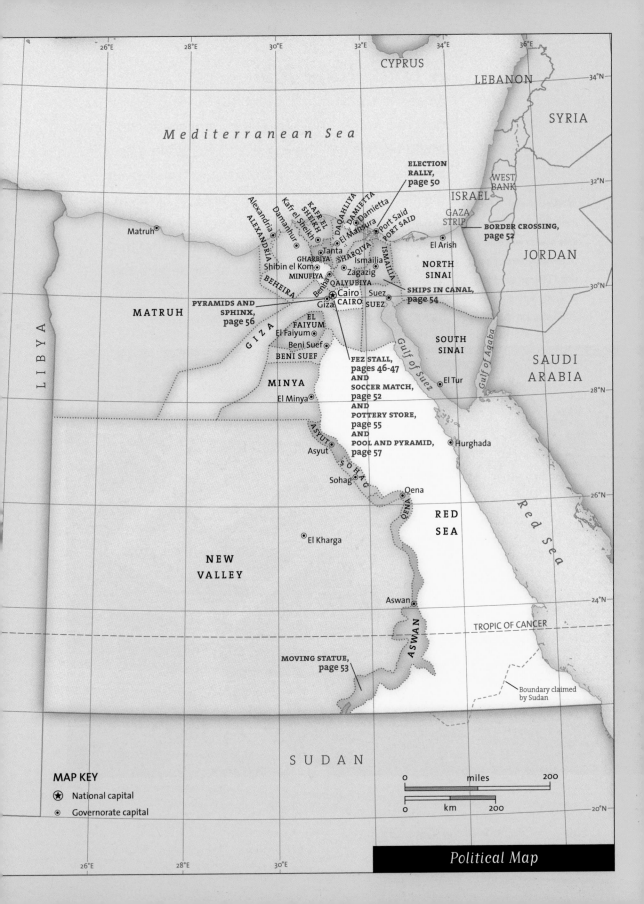

CYPRUS

LEBANON

SYRIA

Mediterranean Sea

ELECTION
RALLY,
page 50

ISRAEL

WEST
BANK

GAZA
STRIP

JORDAN

BORDER CROSSING,
page 52

Matruh

Alexandria

Damanhur

Kafr el Sheikh

KAFR EL
SHEIKH

DAQAHLIYA

DAMIETTA

Damietta

Port Said

PORT SAID

El Arish

ALEXANDRIA

El Mansura

Tanta

GHARBIYA

SHARQIYA

Ismailia

ISMAILIA

NORTH
SINAI

Shibin el Kom

MINUFIYA

Zagazig

BEHEIRA

Benha

QALYUBIYA

Cairo

Suez

SHIPS IN CANAL,
page 54

PYRAMIDS AND
SPHINX,
page 56

CAIRO

Giza

SUEZ

Suez

MATRUH

GIZA

EL
FAIYUM

El Faiyum

SOUTH
SINAI

Gulf of Suez

Gulf of Aqaba

SAUDI
ARABIA

Beni Suef

BENI SUEF

FEZ STALL,
pages 46-47
AND

El Tur

MINYA

SOCCER MATCH,
page 52
AND

El Minya

POTTERY STORE,
page 55
AND

ASYUT

POOL AND PYRAMID,
page 57

LIBYA

Asyut

SOHAG

Hurghada

Sohag

Qena

El Kharga

QENA

Qena

RED
SEA

Red Sea

NEW
VALLEY

Aswan

TROPIC OF CANCER

ASWAN

MOVING STATUE,
page 53

Boundary claimed
by Sudan

SUDAN

MAP KEY

⊛ National capital

⊙ Governorate capital

| 0 | miles | 200 |

| 0 | km | 200 |

Political Map

A Long-Time Job

Since the creation of the republic in 1952, Egypt has only had four presidents. The current president, Hosni Mubarak, has had the job since 1981. One reason is because only one candidate was ever put forward by the People's Assembly for the public to approve. The public vote made little difference. Few political parties were legal. Many Egyptians complained that the system had to change in order to modernize the economy and attract money from abroad, which would help solve problems like high unemployment.

▼ Presidential candidate Ayman Nour gets a noisy welcome from supporters of his El Ghad (Tomorrow) Party at a rally during the 2005 election campaign.

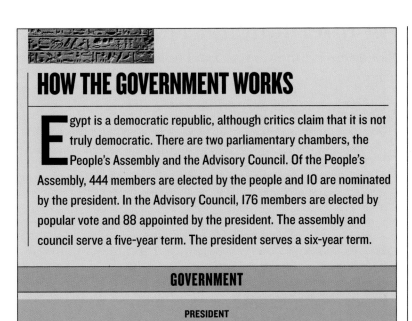

HOW THE GOVERNMENT WORKS

Egypt is a democratic republic, although critics claim that it is not truly democratic. There are two parliamentary chambers, the People's Assembly and the Advisory Council. Of the People's Assembly, 444 members are elected by the people and 10 are nominated by the president. In the Advisory Council, 176 members are elected by popular vote and 88 appointed by the president. The assembly and council serve a five-year term. The president serves a six-year term.

GOVERNMENT

PRESIDENT

PEOPLE'S ASSEMBLY	ADVISORY COUNCIL

In 2005 Mubarak announced that for the first time more than one candidate could run for president. The election that year was the most exciting ever. People marched in the streets in support of politicians who opposed Mubarak's National Democratic Party (NDP). But there were still restrictions on who could run for president, and many people did not bother to vote. When Mubarak won the election easily, they claimed that the result was rigged.

A new People's Assembly was also elected in 2005. The NDP won another majority, but there were significant changes. Members of the Muslim Brotherhood, an Islamic party outlawed in the 1950s for its use of violence, ran as independent candidates. They won 20 percent of the seats.

▼ Hosni Mubarak has worked hard to keep peace between Egypt's Arab neighbors and Israel. The policy has made him unpopular: He has survived two assassination attempts.

An International Player

Since signing the Camp David agreement with Israel in 1978, Egypt has played a key role in the search for peace between Israel and Palestine. Egypt has been host to numerous conferences to discuss the problem. In 2004, Egypt worked closely with Israel and the Palestinian Authority to ensure stability after Israel withdrew from Gaza, on the border with Egypt.

After Israel briefly invaded Lebanon in 2006 to capture terrorists based there, the Egyptians offered support for the Lebanese in a fitting way for two sports-obsessed countries. The Egyptian soccer team—the African champions—played a friendly game against a team from different Arab nations representing Lebanon to raise money for people affected by the fighting.

▼ Egyptian taxicabs wait to cross the border into the Palestinian territory of Gaza. Egyptians have great sympathy for their neighbors, who have at different times been governed against their will by Israel.

▶ The Egyptian soccer team (red) lines up with the Lebanon team, which included stars from throughout the Arab world, in 2006. The Egyptians won 7–0.

THE ASWAN HIGH DAM

▲ Workers move the face of one of the giant statues of Ramses from the temple of Abu Simbel.

In ancient times Aswan marked the southern border between Egypt and its neighbors. In modern times, it has become famous as the site of a remarkable feat of engineering. The Aswan High Dam was completed in 1971 to store the floodwaters of the Nile River. For the first time in history, Egyptians could control the mighty river. They could make water available to farmers in the dry season, enabling them to grow two or more crops a year. However, the dam also traps silt, preventing it from fertilizing the Nile Valley as it had done for millennia. Farmers now rely on artificial fertilizers.

Behind the massive dam lies the 310-mile (500-km) Lake Nasser, which stretches across the border into Sudan. As the lake rose, its waters threatened the Temple of Abu Simbel, carved into a cliff by the king Ramses II over three thousand years ago. The temples and their huge statues of the king were carefully sawed into pieces, moved, and reassembled on an artificial hill about 650 feet (200 m) farther west. They are still one of the most popular tourist sites on the Nile.

Developing Economy

Compared to Western countries in North America and Europe, wages in Egypt are low. Living standards are rising, however. Government measures to move industry from state control into private ownership have boosted the economy.

Agriculture is also vital. It relies on *fellahin*, or farmers who work plots of land in much the same way as their ancestors. Up to a third of the labor force works on farms, growing rice, onions, and citrus fruit

THE SUEZ CANAL

The Suez Canal, which joins the Mediterranean Sea to the Indian Ocean, has made Egypt one of the most important countries in the world in terms of transportation. The canal opened in 1869 as a shortcut between Europe and Asia, saving ships the long journey around South Africa. It was of great importance to the French and British, providing a gateway to their colonies in the East.

Mediterranean Sea

Nile Delta

Port Said

El Arish

Suez Canal

Ismailiya

Benha

Great Bitter Lake

Cairo

Suez

Nile

Gulf of Suez

0 mi 40

0 km 40

During World War I (1914–1918) and World War II (1939–1945) Britain fought to prevent the canal from falling into enemy hands. When Egypt's President Nasser took control of it in 1953, during a standoff with the British and French known as the Suez Crisis, it was a major achievement for the Arab world and a blow to the old European empires.

Today, some 50 ships pass through the canal every day. They pay about $3 billion in fees to Egypt every year.

▶ Ships take about eleven hours to sail through the canal.

for export. Farms also provide cotton for export and for Egypt's largest manufacturing industry, textiles. But even with irrigation and the use of fertilizers, the land does not produce enough food for Egypt's growing population. Some crops have to be imported.

The government would like to modernize agriculture, but many farmers cannot afford to buy the new equipment they need to get the most out of their land. One solution is to create more land by reclaiming parts of the desert. Major development projects are using canals to carry water from the Nile into the desert.

Egypt is rich in natural resources. The desert may be barren in terms of growing crops, but it has reserves of oil and gas that make up Egypt's largest export. There are other hidden treasures, too, such as iron ore and

chromium. Salts from evaporated desert lakes are used to make fertilizers, and the outcrops of limestone in the desert are mined to make cement.

Small Businesses

Although industry is becoming modernized, Egypt is still largely a country of small businesses. Downtown streets are often lined not just with stores but with workshops where people repair shoes, tires, bikes, and cars. Hawkers sell almost anything. The bazaars can be exciting and noisy places as hawkers' shouts mix with the sound of customers haggling over prices and the noise from workshops. Some of the traders make a living by selling souvenirs to tourists. Other street entrepreneurs wait to offer their services as guides, or to do odd jobs for local people.

INDUSTRY

Egypt's industry is based in a few centers and is mainly related to processing valuable natural resources to make products such as chemicals and cement.

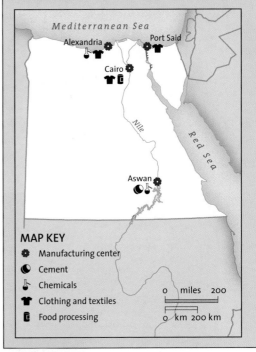

MAP KEY
- Manufacturing center
- Cement
- Chemicals
- Clothing and textiles
- Food processing

◀ **Women chat outside their pottery store in the bazaar of Old Cairo.**

Thriving Tourism

Despite its oil and gas exports, Egypt's largest single source of foreign income is tourism. Since the 19th century, visitors have flocked to see ancient monuments such as the Great Pyramids and the Sphinx, or to enjoy the sights of Cairo. In 1869 Egypt was the destination of the first tour arranged by Thomas Cook, whose company is today one of the world's biggest travel agents. The trip marked the creation of the modern idea of a vacation, and opened Egypt to mass tourism.

▲ The great sites of ancient Egypt, such as the pyramids and the Sphinx, are famous all around the world—and appear on stamps as symbols of Egypt itself.

Today, a new tourist area has grown up on the Red Sea. The combination of sunshine, warm seas, and diving to explore the coral reefs attracts thousands of visitors. Officially, tourism in Egypt supports only 150,000 registered workers, a tiny share of the country's workforce. But that figure does not include the army of informal workers who also rely on tourists, such as camel drivers, guides, and hawkers.

A Powerful Attraction

One problem of relying on income from tourism is that it can be difficult for the government to predict how many people will visit the country. The figure varies from year to year. It drops when there is trouble in the Middle East, such as the 2003 invasion of Iraq, for example. It also falls after attacks within Egypt itself by Islamic terrorists. Tourists soon return after trouble, however. It seems that people from all over the world will always be eager to come to see the treasures of Egypt.

▼ Modern tourist developments now surround many of Egypt's ancient treasures, which some visitors think spoils their atmosphere.

Add a Little Extra to Your Country Report!

I f you are assigned to write a report about Egypt, you'll want to include basic information about the country, of course. The Fast Facts chart on page 8 will give you a good start. The rest of the book will give you the details you need to create a full and up-to-date paper or PowerPoint presentation. But what can you do to make your report more fun than anyone else's? If you use your imagination and dig a bit deeper into some of the topics introduced in this book, you're sure to come up with information that will make your report unique!

>Flag

Perhaps you could explain the history of Egypt's flag, and the meanings of its colors and symbols. Go to **www.crwflags.com/fotw/flags** for more information.

>National Anthem

How about downloading Egypt's national anthem and playing it for your class? At **www.nationalanthems.info** you'll find what you need, including the words to the anthem in Arabic and English, plus sheet music for the anthem. Simply pick "E" and then "Egypt" from the list on the left-hand side of the screen, and you're on your way.

>Time Difference

If you want to understand the time difference between Egypt and where you are, this Web site can help: **www.worldtimeserver.com**. Just pick "Egypt" from the list on the left. If you called Egypt right now, would you wake whomever you are calling from their sleep?

>Currency

Another Web site will convert your money into pounds, the currency used in Egypt (also sometimes known as guinays). You'll want to know how much money to bring if you're ever lucky enough to travel to Egypt: **www.xe.com/ucc**.

>Weather

Why not check the current weather in Egypt? It's easy—simply go to **www.weather.com** to find out if it's sunny or cloudy, warm or cold in Egypt right this minute! Pick "World" from the headings at the top of the page. Then search for Egypt. Click on any city you like. Be sure to click on the tabs below the weather report for Sunrise/Sunset information, Weather Watch, and Business Travel Outlook, too. Scroll down the page for the 36-hour Forecast and a satellite weather map. Compare your weather to the weather in the Egyptian city you chose. Is this a good season, weather-wise, for a person to travel to Egypt?

>Miscellaneous

Still want more information? Simply go to National Geographic's One-Stop Research site at **http://www.nationalgeographic.com/onestop**. It will help you find maps, photos and art, articles and information, games and features that you can use to jazz up your report.

Glossary

Afterlife the state of existence in which the Egyptians thought the dead lived on.

Book of the Dead a collection of spells buried with the dead to protect them in the afterlife.

Canal an artificial waterway built either to provide water for irrigation or for transportation by boat.

Cultivation preparing soil for planting crops.

Delta a fan-shaped area where a river divides into many channels where it meets the sea.

Ecosystem a community of living things and the environment they interact with; an ecosystem includes plants, animals, soil, water, and air.

Extinct a species that has died out.

Habitat the environment where an animal or plant lives.

Haggle to bargain in order to agree on a price between a trader and a customer.

Irrigate to artificially water dry land to make it suitable for farming.

Marginal land land on the edge of the wilderness that can be used for farming but is not very fertile.

Medieval of the Middle Ages, from about 476 to 1453.

Migration the repeated, usually seasonal, travels of animals (including humans) from one place to another in search of food, better weather, and better conditions in which to raise young.

Minaret a tall thin tower attached to a mosque from which the muzzein calls Muslims to prayer.

Mosque a holy building used by Muslims for worship.

Moulid a festival to mark the birthday of a saint or other holy figure.

Mummification preserving a body by removing its organs, drying it, and sometimes wrapping it in layers of cloth.

Muslim a follower of the Islamic religion.

Nomads people who do not live in a permanent home but move from place to place, usually seasonally.

Pan-Arabism a belief that all Arabic peoples should have shared political and religious aims, whatever country they come from.

Peninsula land that is nearly surrounded by water.

Pith soft material found inside a plant stem.

Plateau a large, relatively flat area that rises above the surrounding land.

Pyramid a four-sided structure with a square base that rises to a point. The Egyptians used pyramids to bury their rulers and other important people.

Scavenge to feed off trash and other waste.

Species a type of organism; animals or plants in the same species look similar and can only breed successfully among themselves.

Wetland land that is usually soaking wet or covered by shallow water.

Bibliography

Badawi, Cherine. *Footprint Egypt*. New York: Footprint Handbooks, 2004.

Baines, John, and Jaromir Malek. *The Cultural Atlas of Ancient Egypt*. New York: Facts on File, 2006.

http://www.ancientegypt.co.uk/menu.html
(British Museum Ancient Egypt site)

http://www.historyforkids.org/learn/egypt/index.htm
(Ancient Egypt index)

http://www.sis.gov.eg/En/Default.htm
(Egypt State Information Service)

http://inic.utexas.edu/menic/Countries_and_Regions/Egypt/
(useful links to a range of sites)

Further Information

NATIONAL GEOGRAPHIC Articles

Fahmy, Dalia. "Cairo Current." NATIONAL GEOGRAPHIC TRAVELER (March 2006): 34–35.

Hawass, Zahi. "Curse of the Pharaohs: My Real-Life Brush With Mummy Magic." NATIONAL GEOGRAPHIC KIDS (May 2004): 32–33.

Humphreys, Andrew, and Paul Martin. "Into an Antique Land." NATIONAL GEOGRAPHIC TRAVELER (March 1999): 96–113.

Kirsch, Melissa. "Cairo, Egypt: Grazing in the Grand Bazaar." NATIONAL GEOGRAPHIC TRAVELER (May/June 2003): 104.

McRae, Michael J. "Chasing the Nile." NATIONAL GEOGRAPHIC ADVENTURE (May 2004): 40.

Musgrave, Ruth. "Go On Safari! Destination: Africa." NATIONAL GEOGRAPHIC KIDS (September 2006): 38–39.

Price, Sean. "Treasures of the Tomb." NATIONAL GEOGRAPHIC KIDS (November 2002): 21.

Rattini, Kristin Baird. "King Tut's Mysterious Death." NATIONAL GEOGRAPHIC KIDS (August 2005): 32–36.

Wiwa, Ken. "Free Speech." NATIONAL GEOGRAPHIC (September 2005): Geographica.

Web sites to explore

More fast facts about Egypt, from the CIA (Central Intelligence Agency):
https://www.cia.gov/cia/publications/factbook/geos/eg.html

Look inside the pyramids and learn how they were built:
http://www.nationalgeographic.com/pyramids

The Egyptian Ministry of Tourism welcomes you with all sorts of information about Egypt:
http://www.touregypt.net/

Want to know more about Egypt's national parks? Try the Egyptian Environmental Affairs Agency:
http://www.eeaa.gov.eg/protectorates/

For all sorts of questions about Ancient Egypt, the Oriental Institute at the University of Chicago will have the answer. Select "Egypt" in the box marked "For Students":
http://oi.uchicago.edu/OI/DEPT/RA/ABZU/YOUTH_RESOURCES.HTML (case sensitive)

Index

Credits

Picture Credits

Front Cover—Spine: Stephen St. John/NG Image Collection; Top: Richard Nowiz/NG Image Collection; Lo far left: Kenneth Garrett/NG Image Collection; Lo left: O. Louis Mazzatenta/ NG Image Collection; Lo right: Fridmar Damm/Zefa/Corbis; Lo far right: Jodi Cobb/NG Image Collection.

Interior—Corbis: Johannes Armineh/Sygma: 44 up; Shawn Baldwin: 50 lo; Christie's Images: 33 lo; Gianni Dagli Orti: 32 up; Paul Hardy: 2–3, 24–25; Charles & Josette Lenars: 59 up, 59 center; Neil Marchand/ Liewig Media Sport: 45 lo; David Rubinger: 35 lo; Mohammed Saber/EPA: 52 center; Getty Images: AFP: 52 lo; Time Life Pictures: 49 lo; NG Image Collection: Thomas J. Abercombie: 31 up, 54 lo; Jonathan Blair: 18 lo; Jodi Cobb: 5 up, 43 up, 51 lo; Bill Ellzey: 2 left, 6–7, 28 up; Kenneth Garrett: 3 left, 12 lo, 20 lo, 21 lo, 26 up, 29 up, 29 center, 29 lo, 36–37, 42 up, 42 lo, 43 lo, 45 center; Martin Gray: 15 up; Georg Gerster: 53 up; Beverly Joubert: 23 lo; O. Louis Mazzatenta: 40 up; George F. Mobley: 13 up; Klaus Nigge: 22 lo; Richard Nowitz: TP, 10 up, 11 up, 30 lo, 56 up, 57 up; Winfield Parks: 10 lo, 55 up; Carsten Peter: 15 lo; Reza: 14 center; James L. Stanfield: 2 right, 16–17, 23 up, 31 lo, 34 up, 41 lo; Stephen St. John: 3 right, 46–47, 56 lo.

Text copyright © 2007 National Geographic Society
Library edition ISBN: 978-1-4263-0027-1
First paperback printing 2009
Paperback ISBN: 978-1-4263-0572-6
Published by the National Geographic Society.

For more information, please call 1-800-NGS-LINE (647-5463) or write to the following address:

NATIONAL GEOGRAPHIC SOCIETY
1145 17th Street N.W.
Washington, D.C. 20036-4688 U.S.A.

Visit the Society's Web site at www.nationalgeographic.com

Printed in the United States of America

Series design by Jim Hiscott.
The body text is set in Avenir; Knockout.
The display text is set in Matrix Script.

Front Cover—Top: Young guests at a hotel on the outskirts of Cairo play soccer in front of the pyramids at Giza; Low Far Left: Gold death mask of King Tutankhamun; Low Left: Felucca sailing on the Nile; Low Right: Night view of Cairo; Low Far Right: A camel and its owner at a camel market in Cairo.

Page 1—Camels pass the pyramids of Giza; Icon image on spine, Contents page, and throughout: Ancient Egyptian hieroglyphics.

09/WOR/1

Produced through the worldwide resources of the National Geographic Society

John M. Fahey, Jr., *President and Chief Executive Officer*; Gilbert M. Grosvenor, *Chairman of the Board*; Nina D. Hoffman, *Executive Vice President, President of Book Publishing Group*

National Geographic Staff for this Book

Nancy Laties Feresten, *Vice President, Editor-in-Chief, Children's Books*
Bea Jackson, *Director of Design and Illustration*
Virginia Koeth, *Project Editor*
Lori Epstein, *Illustrations Editor*
Stacy Gold, Nadia Hughes, *Illustrations Research*
Carl Mehler, *Director of Maps*
Priyanka Lamichhane, *Assistant Editor*
R. Gary Colbert, *Production Director*
Lewis R. Bassford, *Production Manager*
Maryclare Tracy, Nicole Elliott, *Manufacturing M...*

Brown Reference Group plc. Staff for this Bo...

Designers: Alan Gooch, Dave Allen
Picture Manager: Becky Cox
Maps: Martin Darlinson
Artwork: Darren Awuah
Index: Kay Ollerenshaw
Senior Managing Editor: Tim Cooke
Design Manager: Sarah Williams
Children's Publisher: Anne O'Daly
Editorial Director: Lindsey Lowe

About the Author

SELINA WOOD studied for her BA in history at the University of Leicester, United Kingdom, before moving to London, where she has worked for 12 years as an editor and writer of children's books. She is the author of a wide range of illustrated titles for young readers, from picture books to informative books on looking after animals and children's health issues.

About the Consultants

PROFESSOR JERE L. BACHARACH taught Middle East history at the University of Washington, Seattle, WA, for almost forty years. He has authored and edited numerous books and articles, including *A Middle East Studies Handbook* and *Islamic History through Coins*. Bacharach served as president, Middle East Studies Association, and twice as president, Middle East Medievalists. He was also president, Association of Professional Schools of International Affairs.

MR. USAMA SOLTAN is currently a Visiting Instructor of Arabic at Middlebury College, Vermont, where he teaches both Arabic and linguistics courses. Born and raised in Egypt, he received his BA and MA degrees in English from Ain Shams University, Cairo, before studying for a Ph.D in linguistics at the University of Maryland, College Park. Mr. Soltan's research has been presented at several international conferences in the U.S. and Europe, and in publications on Arabic language and linguistics.